Dream Boat
FIRST EDITION

Copyright © 2020 Shelley Feller
All rights reserved
Printed in the United States of America
ISBN 978·1·7348167·0·9

DESIGN ≈ SEVY PEREZ
Adobe Caslon Pro, Joy Pixels, Fixture, & Helvetica

This book is published by the

Cleveland State University Poetry Center
csupoetrycenter.com
2121 Euclid Avenue, Cleveland, Ohio 44115-2214

and is distributed by

SPD / Small Press Distribution, Inc.
spdbooks.org
1341 Seventh Street Berkeley, California 94710-1409

A CATALOG RECORD FOR THIS TITLE IS
AVAILABLE FROM THE LIBRARY OF CONGRESS

Shelley Feller

"Thirst's all-in-all in all a world of wet."

Gerard Manley Hopkins

glo-baude

ack

irradiant lure

the is little scene   to be with   feed with
workfool feel to spree which   intimate nothing
i fester with my sex

i be langue in my glow bod no bod   halving my
self   in the haha process   hark!
i   panky wanton in the landscape   ¡scram!

whatever i am   i don't want it in bed with me

hornty oughtn't   o we-machine
this prissy peephole lores
raid unafraid & happy circumference

all civic stink sprung
from my evil smelling hole
behold   the shame-on-me-crazy   yes-
ing-ly yieldeth
everywhere is silver private fun & automatic but not everywhere   equally   everywhere is silver
but   not everywhere   a little loch   a lozenge   is   everywhere is   is
silver   but   is the quite-alone   equally   not   everywhere is   i
muscle-up & mouth-around
silver   but not everywhere   everywhere is silver   but not everywhere
equally   everywhere is silver normal wormhole but   not   equally   everywhere is
silver   but   not everywhere   our masked & plush exclosure   equally   everywhere is
silver   but
equally   in the sump & in the symptom   dumping ontic   not
everywhere is
silver   but   not everywhere   equally
everywhere is   silver   but   not   satyr lickers blister
everywhere   is silver   but   mutable mutual bodies

tinny ingot of my inmost invert   i wore my was
in the whim   < sissy missile >
¡morph!

my monstered dirt   in time did rot

what took root   a cute universe of work

9

why not pirate

paradise?

is is living-philic
in the sunk
& in the sinking

behold   this litmus of longing

our sudden sun

& distant dosage

i fatten my fleet/ i pray for meat

ack, immaculate suite of vast & sensate citizenry

satellite, secrete
indocile simulant in globules

lala thotty got ghouly day-glo monstr'd

decrepit, delicious, deodorant
our lush & distant risk
in liquid orbs contam

pusillanimous animal, dissimulate

i am chrono-fucking the input cam, o
plentiful fulcrum, unzipped
& suckering sacrifice

i got heaven along

i got heavy alone

in vino vanitas tasseled inglorious
gore & greasing our beastly
wee & brunting on 'em

my heart's in my hand
& my hand is pierced

what i am's endued ample
dithyrambic sissitude
i make sissssy on ye
i spake sissy on ye
satyr krater, contam!
contam, antsy stamen, i am
mmmmashing in perpetuity

bedazzled bedeviled benuked denuded
extruding soupçons of—

spamblockhamhockglamrocksmallsprachmanmach
ramrodclamstocksmellsmockhemlockcamcockshell
shockhotspotcumsockjockrotfanbotfatfophandjob
scramglockscram

i am going thru the wormhole
our bloated throat & quantum foam
♫ i feel love ♫
en l'air terrif—our threshold
enfleshed & many-dawned

i am *so* getting heaven along

i vibe my own open organ
distend all present portent
our scrummed industrious
blunt bred & stank

desist, dissolute, depilatory

i prinker sip-simper, swabbed
abaft hatch of—filleted
& braying in the nectary

the outside
i go all the way around

how not to be seen

flensed & eking there
all formal feelers
the horizon, i display/ displace
nothing, nonlinear slit & slip
as too touch our shred remembered
tuck't & corpulent torquing the field
i's slimy mattering
i am shaving, dear crater craver
begat vectoring fatty fleurs
ack-ack, informatic
i seize the means of
calibrate/ liquidate
i am the quite-quite exclusive extrusion
shut
my hand's in the bag, and the bag is
xenomorphic matrix
inducing it, scoping it
i traverse the squirmhole

fleet week! cum manned me in the hows of warship

free-ball hee-haw phony shun, uhhh forked nigh stud
for god on thigh of lolz, ham a peeped seizer swole
spanned his prophet manned boss.
            ack. horrend unders me
fact his bones in whimpers. assy brosé sin cells
the capsid the phages offed his fey twink coot
bent or swing the twirl't fool.
            gentle or cruel
o youyou turnt ha wheelies unhooked o whimwart,
cum sitter flea bus, who was once manxome and jaundiced too.

s.o.s. girl overboard

depending on how you read a thing/ the ship is free, or it is sinking

aye, ich icky thicc physic, suck-o

i'm a snack, natch
stabbed of thee, ye lech

i dress't, deliver't the victual

aclang, acock, atop, agog
i got yr gog adance, adangle

delectable undetected deee-lite

belay that mister-man—an anagram of chiasmus
—i chum ass

fuddy rudder main-topgallant backstays all spanker gaff
crossjack in the companionway—get slushed
lubberly ~~whaling~~ wailing lousey fo'c'sle head
bottleful-handsome yawping jolly

kick off ye leaky sea-boots
licky bucko in the footropes, loose fast
—hoise yrself

hungover sun, i bon voyage
guns out, sun over yardarm

      ♬ i swill, i swish upon me men
            to tease and tarry, treat them
                  in a decent way, grog them
                        all three times a day ♬

are gay? ay, it's a lick it up opry !

~~a rose will bloom, it then will fade~~

eros' ill boom, fit men parade

(rotated text, upside-down:)

ablow abide
aport accurst athwart abloom aboard abreast abut aback
a rum a room a rémoulade
awreck
awaste awash awave away aweather wheels awhirl awrong

alive alive alive alive i shrine the quiet
corps of ghosts

that lake the eyes   aloof

  touching/not touching my loof

bussy gussied & gilt, we bust
we break for better weather
        bent am ich to dog

·S·O·S·   ·S·O·O·S·

                ·S·O·S·

♫ haul upon the bowline, the bowline haul
        the beau's'n brawls in sloe gin's thrall
            sweeter than honey & bitter as gall
                tack't to windward, sin-song's squall ♫

        ·S·O·S·

                                        ·S·O·S·

                ·S·O·O·S·

oh, ich, all ought to sin in   ·S·O·S·

atone, gay fug! we holystone
we hose a rogue, our bloated soak
we strike a pose & bully blow
we disembark in some snug harbor

15

homeward, hommewart
doily skin of sea

       be lean, be loin, beleaguer
       water is from outer space"

       pelagic belly of wealth, permit me
       voyage, love, into yr hands

strong salt junk
i warp him in

men's bones mince in the tides
　　O shun ye sussy
　　　lapping at their graveholes
where water plays with itself
　　　　ripe-sweet
　　　　& barnacled lesions creep
　　　　　across his flesh like fingers aye
　　　　wet air all wasted whims did blow
　　　　　fat waggery
　　　　big horny zephyr slimes
　　　　sublime legions of men
　　　　in pendant bending arch
　　　　　　held-fast—
　　　　trillion inchling rivets needled
　　　　to a point
　　　　　　cleaved—

　　　　　　　　　　horizon's he-machine
　　　　　　　　　　stinking of seamen

♫ let the rain fall down ♫

　　　　　　　　ye drownt ye drooping
　　　　　　what err a body swallowed
　　　　　　did come again
　　　　　　thunderheads
　　　　　　　　it flow
　　　　　　　　it flow it
　　　　　　　　　crash
　　　　right through the gates
　　　　of wrath
　　　　　　rightthruthegatesofwrath

Offed'm discreet (tut tut)   he-lathe whyyy'd ~~a shrum the~~ sludge   *I have seen the Word*
his edge dissect   boffo(!)   sof'ly drownt blown homme   he-saw behemoth(o!)   ~~made~~ *Flesh I mean*
~~infectiously~~ ecstasy screed err(!)   numb heir is he-botch   *nothing less and I know*
fleet on ye lusty war   manned whirrs blub skewered—   *now that there is such a*
              stabbed of thee ye leek   *thing as indestructible*

in tandem rex! (tut tut)   ghast it lout—zounds!   offal belles   *where sex is*
thuck(!)   gay ich of death   mount the living lack   *all grotto, lo!*   *beaten out—*
battered   chapped ere hid id's ugly glitch~~is~~ *living in the shadow of that bride*   *multitude of*
his organs bloomed ink   where aye dare ~~spunk~~ scruff ye spells   *humiliations*
                                            in this reality
men won the cirque-het homme ~~sprung~~ slung cess-spoil   *promise*
slit'm (tut tut)   thy lassoed'n farmed ~~calamus~~ manned-malice wrecked'm wiled *i feel the future*
frost-dead   i scare-wart fat-fatty   Lyft'd mallster's   *the ecstasy*
canticle psy-bent nancies   crypt ich roused he-spars *all topmast he think, as if!* *of walking hand in*
                                        hand across the most
rumpus squadron dandles hex-bent bussy-blithe   *beautiful   world*
non! martyr vibes nigh wilde inner erasure   creeps   *I have never walked*
no-homo-me (tut tut)   doll smut ~~spank~~ spake the ~~mariner~~ marionette   *and never can walk*
his fab-boo joie shallow on ye suss secretes   *with another*

                                        S.O.S.

blotto-blotto   plunder yonder lubber   what err a body weathered seas-me other

blub-hot   ensorcelled asunder

             O   shun ye sussy   lapping at my gravehole

O shun ye foul-foul   O shun ye foul foul foul foul

~~we glitter swift horrif~~
~~we glitter swift horrif~~
~~we glitter swift horrif~~
~~we glitter swift horrif~~

after the fall

i put the anal back in bacchanal

i descend the tender foul
all false fruit & bitter butter

bunker hunk, i lubba lub u
hot like bone broth, jock rot

o, humanimal, i am
hostile to ur harp & altar

i wanna rassle, "no homo"
rassle gracile, sussy

      u duckwalk unto me
      as i duckwalk unto u

   blundered onto love   ♫ding dong♫

i vibe my own doting omen
rode that dormant organ down

all gay ethic, eh?

totes cavorted loosey auf blues atop drone of you
tucked a diabolic no to sport ((o evidence))
against unleavened ass

comme ça

~~can pass alright~~
by thee hygienic apparatus

the fugacity of life's pleasures/ infatuate, fatty cutlet!

heck yes yer ghost gets hosed au jus
smear of nude glucoser & closer
garçon got fat gathered all good
hot on hormonal goo rune
he-man spit dip, lick ich hickey-sigil doh!
dewy-glee today o throne me! crush all
muscle-scruff, organic ultra facial toner, de-
odorant, gas-x, xanax, loose a rude
toot, fruit-of-the-loom hunk snooze
in ruddy bloom, lube up some silicone
props, pop-top & pivot dip anoint
oozing *fffffth* induce adieu
smock off blithe oil for men prepare
barbican barbasol barbarella, charméd waters burn

♫ **butchered so nightly, yet love me** ♫

aooga! bully for me o what nerve!
lack-a-dei / cum manned
me in the hows of warship!
little god got can't body
wont body / i's aw was   what nerve!   what nerve!
sum snug harbor huh sess! mixed reality   beefcake
          zine queen   sea sick

eff'n cake / uhh très fem
cake ~~evades~~ diabolic   Fleet® what nerve! what
boulevards / always obsession   abscessed &
operates ~~in outer boroughs~~   suppurating
outside the ouroboros w.
elemental NO to johnny   what nerve!   dumb hung & 21
5-0 / ~~operates its~~ own *tsk*   saline enema XTC
tsk force w. vascular s: what nerve what nerve!   frosted tips
tsss k   tsss k. fuck'em
suck'em sibilants do the pierced nips tar pits
persons of interest in sissy   what nerve! what nerve
voices what nerve what nerve!   cruise-

young & woozy able vacuoles   dudes in hypno-
the size of body [sized em   sissy ude
up & lo! all topmast they what nerve! is legendary sexy deceased
think [as if!]]
          ENTER mariners   what nerve what
wet: a fleet on fleek & oh! what nerve!   is trap
so *tis of thee*   door   is i licensed   &

synthetic eking there intl mariner
livecams is my public ip & i think it broke inside   what
private semaphore :: ersatz   nerve!
aureola :: â very spiritual
sphincter   aw rooty
            tutti frutti

what a thot–the untold aw rooty
want. now, voyager, sail
thou forth on fleek to grind what nerve!
          what nerve!   what nerve!

     what nerve!

          what nerve!

23

ATLANTIS

bound   arching
be water   by what err it flow it   it crash
        of   syncopate
        yr feelings affect telepathy   the weather in surge & sea
Up   of   granite   steel—
insurgent is a blown't i'd blousey the   is a mist must   i mist i
        must   waveringly   i mist increase my
        liquid assets... god   of   let the rain fall down

through   threading call my drooping my drown't horizontal o blow
arc   of   me home
Their   mouths
bornt me back reply   all   sea in the high-frequency trade winds
                    made
        thy sure all historic weave   ply!
        were winds   is a blown residual hailed,
        every morning & lo from

And   bright   i co-locate
New   the   planar from my outermost
Beyond   frosted   the &
        worlds   raft   of

        rend
White   upward,
With   the induce spars,   the drooping skirt
loft   helm   of my innermost
        like

Slit mouthed around by   light—   a cloud   inter-
cepted way   looms press
        with   tendon
—Tomorrows   link
        cipher-script   reads parades go by   o logical
        through   love
        the   laugh treatment units
                    spears.
                    where the real
hails,   —up
trillion   pink thing feels pain
        sharply
inchling   rivets

you,   hesting
Still sedition urself harness   defensive be
          swarming
        the
ready   believe me   straits!   be
        splintered

levee   be nervous drums,   be
From
          -of-the-
surge
Bridge,   be super   crest surge protected

    deepest   —O   translating
tsunami u gotta   be fluid suns
    what
And   so very   be levee the
                              fuse,
        syllables,
Greedy thy   devising   be-
O   pervasive
leaguered   insurgent   in-

    the   hanging   night
versely perverted illiquid induced   keel.
        lanterns
          end,
be water   be very believe   steel.
    stammer   pangs
    still circular,
me heaven's adaptable   quantum   me-
                      binds—
        wave,
chanical wave shock top   tsunami
          chimes

with nerve steeled   device is   very
O   whose
already in surge & sea   be
    agile
Within   sing
leagues   be low   me bely me
        the
    stars   the   stallion
And ensured belly of wealth water is
        Thou,   sound
          flesh   realm
from outer space clear   in reality is
                      the

bent axiomatic   intrinsic sub   atomic
Swift
shape   secular   out like wet
    unshadow upper ship
  River-throated
ever by what up bright it flow it our
With   swinging crash   ur feelings
don't affect the whether it's getting hot in here
        cities endowed
          ripe so take off

                    all ur clothes   take a dip
                                        sweet
in the pool
                        let's get soaking wet   heart's   farther tides shall not
Forever   glittering   O
contrive   his fabulous
        canticle   chemistry
shallow   LETSGETSOAKINGWET sea born shadows bubble up stone-
        wrapt   and   blinding
sick   ships derelict plundered
thy   prophecy:
                                                    s.o.s. i is there   assailed & sore'd
            spiring
to sunder   sweet-deep eking
        silver   young
ugly worlds   i see.   the sweating horizon
its pinkish meat   i spoil   with my mouth   the real thing is lying
facedown   a sunk stone
        i was alone   & then i was not alone   every mourning & lo
    i co-locate
        Thou   Love.
            this   Flower,
        raft & rend   the weft of me has slipped
            of
Now   suns   us,
(O   its knot   doth   me)   warped   & woofed me under

                floating   LETSGETSOAKINGWET

                                        thy floating song descends
So   beyond
a crypted code ensanguined   tolling   all-in-all in all
That   orphic
a langue lost home
Sidereal   converge:
        Song,   Bridge   Is
        pity   rainbows "o"
        serpent   in
Whispers   in   swing.

on our first date he says he's poz & asks if i'm scared, if i still wanna

+   +   +

i want in want's audience
the so-soft & feminized gasses

of civilization—ah—stags
swarm in synchronicity, a staged

dissection of hard & plush currencies—trade
qua trade on the face of things, i

sit on the face of things, immaculate
the fear the fear the fear the fear—cheer

not the darling pucker
i brother in love's ugly

cutlets, shoveling blub
into my ween-wilde bouche

OOF—finger on my mouse hole
inspected infectious squelching shinola

crying *whát i dó is me: for that i came*
í c'est mórph: the must man's thrust is

is thrall—all in daddy's graces growing
galore, womping galore in my hyperspace

my hyperself—it speaks in spells
ensorcels me—oh—in the moan light

+   +   +

a rose   is   eros   is   arrows

+   +   +

a wormhole opens
& the men who made me

mash—this beasty skin
we species in, stabled

& shorn, blinkered
to moral in ymage's mold

the past—all plastered cast
cracked, & thru the slit comes

a fist of flowers, flaming sworde
deformed transformed—all muscle

sprung to labor love, the rough
factory of flesh invents itself

a ~~representamen~~—fetish'd
& hung scum suckers dumb scruff'd

my rude forensics, pluck up
in the frightened zones

of my theater—meat-slung
selves carried off

in shards—all false heads
of beauty's cooing orphic

anesthetized
a langue lost i

this is a song
& this is too—

butch mercutio first time in drag at capulet ball

beat for the gods, etc
i take it in
sense, feel it, i'm a pretty
piece of flesh, his fish
dipped in ranch

draw thy tool, u man u beast
w. horny rage, yr torture prince
beseeming ornament
          [weird old men depart]
swung his sword & broke wind withal
hiss'd in porn's interpellating
thrust & blow—butthurt, came more&more
till the prince came   O, where is romeo

private in his chamber pens himself
an artificial night so
secret to his bit bud
his wormy sweet sounding
bucking young studs
come, romeo, such is love's transgression
prest & propagated EXEUNT

romeo,   doth thy boff my vex'd & choking sea?
so in sadness, on the DL, do i live dead to tell it?

scruff ye slush-drunk leaky sleazed his cakey pissoir swagger
all haloed rotting lordship, mammalian, and i, by god
so ripely bridal'd, do feed that dogma till i die

horrend   brute feudal'd under

i bade him come & yeah, quoth he, dost thou fall upon thy face?
& yeah, quoth i, then lay yr wormwood to my dug
& in the sun, under dove-house wall, my lord dug
& felt it bitter, pretty fool, with jest & gambol suck'd
a big sore tooth ((tut tut tut)) i know the language, i pray
thee   come, knock and ENTER, & no sooner in
but betook him to his legs & he was done

o senseless cock-a-hoop stick'st in such muck
what have we   in bed asleep i dream'd of you

dumb colt
anon a nonce a nose, you foot it, boy
nuzzled my crupper, sluttish hairs, & smelly pig tail

this is the trick, this is the hag
i lie on my back   expect nothing, beget nothing

~~warts~~ words bloom in spectral legions along our lonely
our pilgrim lips & bitter industry   O trespass
the "weft" of me
has "slipped"
give me my sin
again

of me made paradise algorithm. to lose & be langue, adieu, adieu. anon
brute surely, adieu…i sissy vatic coutured, o, ornament, such sutures. i succor'd under
yer budding governance, & morph, u doth boff my derelict ich! in the surely i scruff'd
"another i is," its little *laaa* thrombotic—hey meathouse, monster-bot got thotty-docile, wonky
off its bloodhole puckered—i gorgonize! ensorcel-unselved, i havoc haute-horrif. lookit, eking
out its living lols, all 'lectric got heaven along! i slut shine vial somatic in my city me manorama

wulp, the sworde u forged me plundered me, smote me under
ruh-roh!! what stern blooming brigade ye, twang ye, honey my many sculptured wonky
shucks. pollution seducing the hole whirled, i *live*, hunty! mounting spirits in my manorama
muscle up to meat me, mute me {sooooey!{ i yips in my is}}, eking
out eternity {rich & juicy} feelies invisible harness, o 'lectric spangled, hark! i scruff'd
sum new cruel & it bored me, did it bad math outside myself "no fatty," all avatar anon

sum grownass raff like lorrdee, can't-fuckingly-drunk scruff'd
hemorrhoids o wino daddy dear u no i was all shuts up sub in my nether manorama
nervy somad in my noisome botcha botcha butthole. i portal sore'd asunder sooooy! lovers wonky
sumpd estrange secret, deep sweet, fleet on ye lusty in surge & sea argonaughty, insurgent anon
o sorrow, my vexed wet zounds. o marrow, row my mariner, my tender'd hide! i shoveled-under
rot a thing so slung that idle i.'s a hole. it come to fill its give. ashore, sweet-deep eking

dizzy ruin't. what men made me brang me in the midst——deveined, divine, i moan ye manorama
i defibrillate mine ymage. repulsal. repulsal. disgust my cyber betchy. ye spread, ye sunder, anon
all godless body, idyll dungeon manacled——eternally {i} kissingly {i} s.o.s. eking
-ly——[i]planetary so mortuary get wreckd {torquing} undress'd duress {ardor, ardor}, i's under
what whether, incite stern pleasure, hark! honky oughtn't me want in want's eye wonky
what big math, unsociable sexy me! cankered & bored ye, muckd & moan ye, wastrel, scruff'd

feelings all ago as bent civic split—silt & sky,
ugly. uglyuglyuglyugly, i wore n/t in the eschaton.
unsearchable thunders, anchor'd[no, know] what
smudging suns. everything is wrong'd, dagger'd
must beyond & bright. terror, this rimless ref-
brüt sissy. i seas in plasticine-sore shallows n/t
lapping at my gravehole. o shun ye foulfoul,
untethered from this, unhomely brush of—beauty,
other {secretes{beating{monotone{ in ecstasy!
my bigbig throne[lustred & orphic] i silk to steepen song
as too touch our shred remembered nothing[this u ur nothing never no{]
wide wet ~~vortex~~ virtue of our hour[immutable[mutual[blood[]

shun ye bridge of—echo's ocean dolls agog, eking
love flooded crest, all immanent scruff'd
death-petalled breast toward harbor pressed under
& sung. sunk rigs live symbiotically, manorama
lection inside me now swarmed {secretes} anon
so pirate as this flaglessly. faggot idyll wonky
ye breed hygienic ontic" {i} fauna nonstop wonky
i's idyll hung a thing so rot that eking
{licit{infection{fringed{ o buttery's[hymmmmn] malade anon
enspelled! thassa pretty sissy mince ayup, scruff'd
ye chummed all swum manorama
in pendant & bending arch numbed under

............muscle-lush
............& muster manorama
............//eons of
//
.........we dream nothing
............feudal'd under
so bloodless, bugaboo....scruff'd/
All
in the wreck room.........
/felt ugly in a field.........felt ugly in a city {bleached} eking
.........ye krater....wonky//beefcake.........{i}
love's living portent...........
{horrend}
brute
.........hex-bent anon.............
............/argonaut

won't be the whole exclusive flesh won't be the marble like that

i walk fat aspic o'thisself on long & zonal strips   pre-fit
to lot us bodies ~~excrementally~~ incrementally
"experience the sluttery life" i am
pageanted in private intervals   i
stop & smell the little things
squirt saline up my anus   i lie in my food
diary app that sells data about my lying
happy pride lol   hole pic?

        everyone knows the parties he danced his mess aground he did all 16 dances
        men r forming roaming all over
        this gl/itchy-injured planet   untethered & bloated
        not of space as it is but of space as we made it, say
        duh'n't it make u feel a whole lot better huh
        smelt a steaming thing soft from my center huh

all gay ethic, eh?

o sussy, i suffer my druthers
gloom gets wreck't w/ pleasure
  soooooooey

goonies & stinkers, lucre'd of gainz
♪ding dong♪
i got goony w/ dongs
i was literal of

all aim in my * damn am i
hypebeasting atrocities, etc.

etcetera perverts all malaperts in verse   ayup

        if fucking is a form of thinking is desire
            susceptible to irony & diseases
            of camp? e.g. yer gaze doth run me thru
            soooooey!
                        sooooey! soooeeeeeeeeeeeeeeeeeeeeeeeeeeEEYY!

            herrrrepiggypiggypiggy here piggy
        herepigpigpigpigPIGGY

yer symptom blunt pulsion to love
ye fuggo
ye wrecked 'em nigh brute future
the figural burden of queerness
is literal of
is felching the 'other' w/in
~~the 'law' is lived as its own transgression~~
disjunctive & copulative
it slicks its hide its baubles uh many good morsel snug in my blub
   y'all, i yawp literal of
heaven is a thing again butt chugging
magnums of Moët
at the fat faggot pageant
  caLLLL the HOGs
this piggy's serving sturgeon, sussy
snuffle up to suck my sac
of roe
so row, ye buttery, brunt drunken milt
sorrow's pricked
w/ pintle's of shame
   are gay?
ay, hanky-spanky ack away & ache
i got BIG HOLE ENERGY
ye argonaughty got doughty by the tankard
despoiled me ~~sequined & scaled~~ scrum-scruff'd & stank
i swish
a pretty mince
i suffer
my druthers
   har!   har-harpoon't
it was literal of
legendary sexy deceased my face
is a flying fish its anus
fleet on ye lusty
the sea jerks off eternally
ye slap i see the sun
   sip sippy
ringed w/ blood around its eye my hole
itching
   sip sippy

                       something was eager for punishment
                               its only recognition

ACK

camp's uh drag

utopic-hungover tradge all pageanted

hip horrif

can pass alright

wuzzat in the lazaret

i

by thee hygienic apparatus

slung back yer sour whack

spent bloomin' screwed   scorbutic   an' crooned

♫ a-rovin's been my ru-eye-in ♫   so row

so row

yer porker ashore

its lovely flesh to chew

*this congealed   ♫ a-cruisin's been my ruuuuuu-in ♫

…skin of   such a messy stew

…shame   what jacuzz!   o sussy

ruptures…

knuckled

…oozes… sick   sweet…

…slime   -under   thumping pucker fat

thuck   in a contagious-identificatory-movement   abaft hatch of

…that is   always-already

i is a backward feeling

hemorrhaging

o marrow me!

…old stancher   wuzzit intimate's   odd mouther

mooning brobaude out lout   in larder

living down the bilge an' livery

o suss ye

shun't   an' lashed to mizzenmast

i kill yer stiffy kissing

-ly

faggots love to lick

...hemorrhoids...   comme ça

    ...sissy-cathected   to death

        ...catharsis   ((catharsissy)) becomes a form of ironic

            queer...contamination...'situating' tragedy   not...

as the antithesis...of camp...but as that which ((camp))

        ...((   )) necessarily 'transgresses'

...in its 'constitution'...

        queer tragedy is uh...   catachresis ((catachresissy))   uhhh... ((threshold

poetics))...

        +   +   +   +

        torquing dominant

...modes...of cultural production &

            revealing instability of 'genre'   & political...

    emotions...embattled...   concealing

        ((all   prolapsed))

    ...& 'face-controlled'

    ...at the club   ...i love

...fashion, etcetera   ...moody bitches do die

  ...for

hanky-spanky ACK away & ache

o rankled, inebriate! all foibles irritate
he-bangle wrangle me ahoy

                                came to

camping in the eschaton   *ahhh*, men
swoon dog doze posing louche
& owning everything

                ♫ shake it up ♫

                           text, corpse, portal   throat, rectum, excrement
                                  metonymic circuits of desire
                                      break—zag, double back—lang-
                    uage folds in precipitous
                   creases accreting grotesque
                       & spectacular ACK   i slit & slick
                  the ~~horizon~~ ((where being surges
              forth ((o congealed o membranous
          i slip pre-lubricated tips i shit
             myself for men they do appeal

      Fleet® on, ye lusty

          i sissy ascesis   i accede
to this nothing

      ♫   ♫

                                    ♫   ♫

amateur drag night/ a fucking didactic

ack-ack, faggot, decant
all chemical splendor
mallets, his eyes, unmake
an instant, this print anatomy
folds like a fancy
for me, it's all about me!!
my chaste & ghoulish
ooooh laa laa laa laa lalala
he-men becometh in me
   (tout de suite!)
feel it fizzingly spinninging
all -ings in line to piss
is preen't & petted on is hornty
warted out my rhinestones
organza, orgasma / contain
contam!! man spat, pat my belly
til i belched, passed gas in my dancy pants
enhancing all the ass i have
(none!)
latch the bathroom—no don't! come
in new youse i attract all
alabaster blast lasher long
-ingly gluey to me—evrythng is i
am gvng u evrythng is
oooooh laa laa laa laa lalala
Alabama's Absolut Icon (!!!)

my gift is my song
& thissun's fer u…

in our oppression
the very structures, that result
& thus reproduce
in the underlying logics,
may themselves be implicated
Acts of resistance

ack-ack, faggot, decant
the dipping sauce
i will attack u cook u in ur jus!
an embarrassment of britches
& oh the stench

& oh the woe man
becometh behemoth in me

got schlong'd, furlong'd & longer got
ooob laa laa laa laa lalala

elicit delicious in all et voilà!

did u stone those tights?
i'll tell ya fer free

desire me make me fire lick licky

trendy ((wig)) ombre ((wig)) balayage ((wig))
backorder blonde ((wig)) gluey blue lagoon
((wig)) crème de menthe ((wig)) cognac lace
front straight up bump it ((wig)) hot unisex
human ((wig)) real top brand believe it ((wig))
whip it pump it serve it ((wig)) just desserts
((wig)) pirouette ((wig)) category is ((wig))
twirl & twirl & twirl & twirl ((wig)) truvada
whore ((wig)) okurrr ((wig)) every boi ((wig))
needs a grrrl ((wig)) needs guidance uniquely
hir own ((wig)) & virgin ((wig)) if classic
((wig)) classy ((wig)) below yer budget
((wig)) if curl ((wig)) hurl ((wig)) showgirl
burl ((wig)) blow yer budget ((wig)) buy now
pay later add to wishlist ((wig)) do you feel
((wig)) that already ((wig)) amp it up ((wig)) a
little ((wig)) to save a life ((wig)) did u stone
((wig)) those tights ((wig))

O, moan ye mussy
no homo no brokeback backdoor bar-back
shablam!
heal fissures with prayer!
organic raw natural organics

gently my joys distill/ lest you break the vessel you should fill

foie! foie! dear fatty
louchely buttered in the eschaton, i sour
thirsting at the seems

                      [cum manned F]: "excess"

shale plays patient math
            fracking daddy calamity
culls polluted transmuter
            shaming me smelly plenty

"i" is nuthin to do with waters! i pump big
feelings into the field to steal[(!!)]

rich & juicy beauty i trigger rapture anon
i, here, now [(seer, etc.)]
vatic avatar dumped a hung chump   (your breath sealed by ghosts   eye dew knot no)

flexure massif shadow, bucko
bogo blush wine & have a care
make pretty ready to

        GO TO COUNTDOWN

footloosing ludes in hypno-sissitude
DANCE, tansy panzer
[(ch)]armed to the teat, i farm hunks
to hunt in my royal forest
in my global porcine holosphere

        GO TO COUNTDOWN

quarry my careful goggling faking it
his frontispiece for pleasant forevers i sigil [(LOL)]
captcha axed off his heir app errant

O, my pretty borehole
i bottom the cruel new nuthin [(zoinks!)]

drinking manxome oh lissomely con cock shuns
une bête blank horror razeth
his ymage, *nonnnnnn*
his palatial BOOGE annexed
verbatim invisible webbing—

what sums sudden crustal 'rupt
rrrrr sugared, urges curtsy verily
astraddle ^(o, sovereign) my pansy scheme

ack, irradiant fleur, ack, happy sacrifice
i sever the stamen inside of—

what took root, butchered
so nightly, yet love me

butchered so nightly, yet love me

O lonely lonely

vassal'd me putrid   ((double membrane

manifest organic factual previsions—

mwah! ally like kissy

inflame, inebriate ((whofrombelow anon

brute sissy bloodlessly

melt *uhhhhn* unwilling & slow

ENTER   ye licky victuals

vessels of dead munition cling

to _____   what skin we

species in   ((in interstitial slits

((crazy horny crazy

s.o.s.

+ + +.

lonely lonely   looonely lonely   yodel-ay-ing

PaStUrE mY aNiMoRpH   i'm rendered remains of

eking me ugly thrussy   o licit psychic ecstasy(!!)

((pink thing i played   in the husbanded place   mmm-
mmmashy, me fleur in my fright zone scruffing mush, bruh

a predator sights all prey in the slew
skinned it wears its lushy bygones like butter

got schlong'd & getting schlong'd, whatever, i take
goo into my head & relaxeth

dabbing oils of ordinary form
my death absorbs ((invisible i
eat, i am worthy, ay, sir i take
my fill of _____

                    ((scat schusses away
extruding sugared plumes   i drinketh
            submersible in mine ~~effluence~~ affluence
i   _lady ladle_   animals ((deep-sweet   i sinketh in fat   ~~ack~~

        ay, flood historic residuals   embark!   ((lol
                                                              ˙s˙o˙s

        all cells become others, endlessly   patrolling
                lonely's replicants   ((acklonelylonely

his Ark is full of bird herpes

daily bugaboo jubilee

i walk 'vance on flattered floor
bragly footing lushy bygones
avant / a lance / a live lost love
i rise nigh / o lucky day / into ru-ayyy-in

prissily nipped / abaft hatch of my thruway
mooning odd mouther / sooooey / savoir faire
my derrière / got down / got lickety literal
verso/ to bear / the brunt / bent & batten i with-

held avast / i / reviled / to mine inner eye
the false brush of beauty / thou polis
in my bosky & in my cervine / i got zonal
w. strangers / assailed me mid-

ship / lowkey exposed recto / ahull of my dead bunghole oculus
baleful rid this how of town chub bucket / lucky day o

contam what lordly animates

ack   at long last

   ass up

            in the office
            of my malefice

o   lackaday
diddle me bibulous

i mollycoddle all comers
i curdle

ship of fools

I.

       the   ruffles
Bright   with
  sweet deep whale as ever   u wheedled
       fingers   of
Gaily my lore and   cajoled my lore   & oh

And   their   little cargo
       lightning
  coaxed out coyly   in the piss earth
  waves   on
    could   me   tell

O i womp u galore   frisk your my cutlet
  shoveling blub   bleached
       elements   is
   must   nor   beyond
Spry   of   caresses
  into my ween-wild bouche wide
  bottom the   cruel

i stomp the ground, grounding
i womp the blub, blubbering

II.

this
rimless   "don't let's ask for the moon"
                    and
       don'ts untold i want to tell   bends
               vast
                        inflections   love   by stars to speak   seek life

     Sea   diapason   land on the moon thou never
On   never never snowy   mooned unwanted sailor   …••
                 terror   rends
                      motion   ill
     the   lovers'
         un-forth un-thou un-sail un-now un-life un-land un-grant un-

     & & &

And   off   "he wishes he understood me   he wishes"
       a sheen on the water lustres   shy oil
In   meadows
Adagios   O   Prodigal   everything unseen beneath our bodies
       hell the yeah fuck die   spell

                    shoulders   our sleazy-sweet planet
  hasten   rich
                   bent   wave   our animal seething   weepie spells
     while   are   well in me   gutter scum   sweltering
                        one
       we's a kind of feeling   songful
       us   O   fffffth   awe thru ur two front teeth
                            fire
                         until   came & got it with ur two front teeth

          in   vortex   our
               wide

49

III.

consanguinity   bears
water come to hole the fill
tendered   that
it give, spill all distant
                                        where
    sudden sprung
            a   wave
rush to fill it up
While   water   I
a body rocking
Are   scattered

        your
by what err it flow
    sea   hands
it crash

ashore sure shock
    so   through

That   otherwise
o, civic virtue
                            lithe
built a fountain that will squirt u
    wrestling   light

    kissing   wave   unto
equip ur lisping sissy kissers
        body
the sea spits dissers in the river
                and   shed

                but
mayday is yadyam
        steep   to
made delicious
    silken   song

as busy as a fizzy sarsaparilla
        me   your

IV.

hours
know   of   pledge
i wore my bouche askance
                parting   gulf
Whose   at a many tossings off
              bridge   palms

                white
              i was the many meanwhile
              of   now
bridging his britches
singing   alone
              aflow   to
on one side, a bridge began
              & also on the other

                                claim
the river was determined
              by its desire to be   this
  region   ours
              eyes   and   determined
                                told
        port   our
              in the many meanwhile was
a man, many men
              bridging their britches
                          and
Bright   and   I
        be   tides tell on the sill of the river
the water became a body
              between silt & sky

                the
        harbor it was & was not his body
Mutual silt, his sky

    widening   your   gathering
        bright piety forbade the river rive
                    my   caught
    islands   & yet its bent
                must
                    levels foam stood & waved

there was a river that took
    this   the sea   exclaim
in its mouth
        oar   of   love

for this the river was   often assailed

V.

past   rime
                    a river is to celebrate its own
                              though
                    division—raft & rend
          merciless

The   hard
          ENTER: the living ~~mariners~~ marionettes
they come inside me now ensorcelled in my blub

As   too   touch
                    they lave my loosing gleeful
          our   swiftly
                    pinking mucosa from inside
          shred   remembered
One   words
                              for i am giant
          this
                    we
                    the hole caboodled

                                        the world end-
                              no
                    ures the ~~whither~~ weather i make
                    this
Slow   moonlight.
                              for now i am giant
          changed
          for now my feelings affect the whether
                    ~~insurgency~~ in surge & sea

Nothing   this   you
                              i womp my flood
                    your
                              i wheedle my flood
     into   cleft
          nothing   dead   flashing
                              i fetter distempered wet

          never   No   but oh—little cargo
                    your   sweet deep
Nothing   as
                    i sorrow my vexed wet zounds

                              so, row…so, row…
                    now
          your   and   sorrow row me homme
eyes   here
                              drifting
                    ashore sweet deep
               by   I
          Draw   head   long   my payday blown
                              home

the sissy in society—powdered painted and laced, they swarm at afternoon teas. thassa sissy, alright, that walk a pretty mince. ensorcel a sissy in thigh high lycra. to sissy is a civic virtue. now, decorate. decorate. decorate. decorate. decorate. decorate. decorate. decorate. decorate. decorate. decorate. decorate.

VI.

decorate. decorate. decorate. decorate. decorate. decorate. decorate. decorate. decorate. decorate.
decorate. decorate. decorate. decorate. decorate. decorate. decorate. decorate. decorate. decorate.

icy   lift
eyes
churning
borders
as   secretes
beating   monotone
as   the
wet
toward
harbor   breast
pressed   the
derelict   blinded

what
let   death
savage   garland

Beyond
The   thunders   away
sail
inmost

thassa pretty sissy mince ayup. chaturbates in tainted lace. decorum assails all swarmed in civic couture. a faggot storm. an F4 faggot storm. paint the town red. lace the town w. AIDS. decorate expectorant in ~~yves saint laurent~~. in ~~versace vers-sausage~~, in ~~comme des fuckdown~~. all faggots love to die. it's death all faggots live for. death is decorated in red. in vestments rending red testament. death is unbetrayable. faggots love treason but love death even more. pop a pretty bussy on the face of death. raze up thy sissy-facial'd nation. now, decorate,

blithe   petalled
the   rose
eyes
unsearchable

decorate. decorate. decorate. decorate. decorate. decorate. decorate. decorate. decorate. decorate.

fervid
Unfolded   before
rainbows   continual
white
imaged   holds

decorate. decorate. desperate. decadent. dilf. dilf. divine.
anchored

It   unbetrayable
no   know

buying spanx at the airport spanx store

trust your thinstincts® & be confident
trust your thinstincts® & being confident, also adjustable

for when nature calls, double gussets
to stopper muffin top

miss muffet in the mirror am coming
   up for air
up and coming phenom bedazzled behemoth
my *hiya daddy* pumiced
   & slick in glamorous spandex, elastane

as seen in *USA Today*

O compressible panoply
of human nylon

   let me touch you

induce municipal licitly tethered to mine own i lay around a while
blithely extruding soupçons of satin, fascial elastin slowwy & farting
   in the body scanner

my whole body is a trouble area
everybody is a trouble area
what marx meant by lumpenproletariat

   imperator begirdled et promptly mort

fatty fatty boombalatty
clogs class concupiscence

thrombotic, O

excess–in compression
socks & thigh high lycra

suck my honky chick-fil-a

happy pride lol hole pic?

in þis dim hol hit habit agin / dis-
gowned all gracile phatic avatar
once vaunted in utmost sissitude / i whirligigged a top
notch gallop / forward the violet of ~~time~~ wine—no, vodka cran
bury yer flimflam tomorrowland / yer debonair en-
cinctured waist depreciates in valor w. every passing

dei / hi, bad. i lied again. dared it out its hole
vocable & round / took its little *aye* behind my back
& torqued it / plaited it / keeled on itching needle
to pleas u / dabba doo u / splash bad w. bravo down diver
in spindrift haze / mayday did ward me zonally
close to zero / so board of yer cycloramic
one story pavilion w. loft above / i was not me
but a fleet of me / sea me waving / half assailed in the whim

if sometimes i seem not here, it's not dreaminess; it's fear

ack, morbid cordial, get ripped, get ribald
trim vim tomorrow's man scans manorama, ahistoric
industrious-numb. scruffing minutest mopings, all the beautifuls buttered
in silhouette. hark, o love-lean, mincing in his undergrowth
i farce bad—splat in the knick of. ~~this is not a cum joke, zoloft~~. i blow sanity
animals into many mini balloons, congrats

i get stabby in my faggy bugaboo jubilee—ack
plastic stallion, i guzzle polluted {ack-ack} google stiletto balloon
barrage, ascendant—o sacral kite, my natal chart inscribes i
dream nothing so flagless as this piracy. spangled dandy, i
suture couture de rigueur—our blood, fatty informatics, evolved as law
gone awol. our legend lives in the between, believes in teeming we's beyond
ha! i wore fear like a hot pink corset. anonymous pommel rode under
him sore'd. ack, dumb bunghole. "i" saddled up somatic
we spree we freely we mutiny, etc.

O

overboard   N

w. sinister hoist NNNON

overboard

    blue peter blue papa

NONON w. sinister hoist ONON

    pole to board o'er ON

blue peter blue papa   N

    w. flag alongside,

pole to board o'er ON

    formed around form-

w. flag alongside,

    less, o romeo   NON

formed around form-

    i'm so bored   NO

less, o romeo

    pratique impractically ON

i'm so bored O

    vassaled me portly

pratique impractically

    no one to stopper N

vassaled me portly NNON

    civil obstruction

no one to stopper

    below the belt, venus ONON

NONON civil obstruction

    unvesseled to fish ON

below the belt, venus

    ginchy astern w. difficulty, leak me clear

unvesseled to fish

    in the see

ginchy astern w. difficulty, leak me clear

    sextant him in the moan light / niner

in the see

    niner sinister NO

sextant him in the moan light / niner

    discharge well in me

niner sinister O

    tactically, down diver

discharge well in me

    to port coursed my alter

tactically, down diver NNON

    my danger nigh & trawling

to port coursed my alter

NONON hoisted high my yankee NON

my danger nigh & trawling

    my dragging rankled

hoisted high my yankee

    anchor, blue papa

my dragging rankled

    blue pilot, keep clear

anchor, blue papa

    i am on fire   NON

blue pilot, keep clear

    i require a tug NO

i am on fire   ON

i require a tug O

N

in the navy

we spree we freely we mutiny
  aye
's a lap it up opry

go langue go lol down in xir ravine
schooner, spoon xir, shoo nor schooled xir, eyed xir
like wine talons, ok? glozed off xir mallets. i's like
smized off xir tinder eyes

reviled returned to you alley-oop
the apple of mine i—all oops
in brüt ecstasy queening! [knock on would]
i's ware it was yew low lowing on yonder
willow rim, exalted in this body's silt, ayup

NEW ANATOMIES!

i's land all garbage garlanded. got me blousey
tossing coin in to yore spout
drop trou & strop me, shocktop. yahweh

NEW THRESHOLDS!

got my goat, alright. pissed
awwicked psaltered homme hey hey
thy taste wine! intercepted be-
clouded got the plumper town gayer
fffffth are thy nuts, sip sippy
in thy licky rocket in the nonstop sippy?
feelings affront the weather. where it flow
it crash. sunk assail

it like look meaningful & deep & slenderizing too—
blue sailor, bunk & ragged horseweed
nipped xir hung root unlobed
plucking succory & bachelor's buttons
a whipped & modest confection
        felt sailor hat, boat-shaped wide-brimmed sailors in white, boys or girls play-hats,
        smart little toasted straw sailor w. floating pink veil, sailor-hatted daphne in a frenzy,
        sailor-man, parcel of sailor-men, sailor shape of chapeau an' i oop—
pet mon petit adieu   ((adieu! adieu!
prissily nipped me ((adieu!

♪♪ O…shun ye suss / sea me savored / in the whim ♪♪

                      i was a wave field   peeling from my center

preen't, breededed an other thresh-
hold to prophet off err's edge
offed others doll agog
echo   *petheticlittlething*

                       ((s.o.s. girl overboard))

fed that dogma til it died
huh

blustered in the win i ball-
oon my sanity raft
fffffth
it was hysteric, onerous, & foul
mwah!
i was dysphoric, odorous, & howl'd
mwah!

ye shing to war me/ har-harpoon

it took microseconds passing through   -ough -ough

so completely going apart   in the be/tween   ay ay

i'm yip yip usurped   in vestment   in red testament rend
-ered   energy leak me light in the clear ~~seas~~   seize   ((press
x to capture   ((x in xxxultry armistice et rex non–
contact aggressor   overrode my little grid

my blis(s)tered horizon O

            i be langue to u

            i do the shuga-loo

            i do all 16 dances

                         ♪ i feel love ♪
                                    ayup

                              it was hip
                              i was hip horrif

contam what lordly animates

luminiferous aether   all lacrimal
avatar is i   ascending the apparatus

what cum-sad animus am odes on
organon organum hors d'oeuvres
enhancing anatomical pouch

smell me a lore, a lure, a bigbig portal glory be
yer true beef hideaway

monsterbot got thotty-docile

yond lunk, u glut vascular relict
masc fer   fey fer
florid in the average field

inebriate, untouchable

i am sloughing off the softer land

~~aster ardor~~   ~~aster ardor~~

cold song

ally like kissy he shovel me under my oils

all fleetling eked my uggo spoils—fat, trans-
muting fat brute futile. use me
he-machine. my d--th absorbs
his ordinary form

for he has made unto me a vessel
of chaos—gently, my joy breaks
the vessel he never
should have filled. O

he father through he drink me out
my holy-useless, my species of not. gaily

animal webbing wore me
spatial, 3-D, vassal'd me yes-ing-ly

—thing that feels—conveyor'd of liquor me drooly
my cordial my breathy *let's living this*
greedy-red-needy wet garment of person

i traitor'd. i blister. i go to him again & again
his dark matter brigade, i
lick he lick he victual munition—dizzy
bids me fey thing vesper'd. i wicked. i
freight in the light like a marble reich

we were evil. anatomical
theater of industrious pleasure

don we now. don we now upon the water what
err dripping triggers my rapturous plenty—*argh*

i scree marauder, yar!
aye, candy for me, screamo rotting goth-hop
my haha wheelies unhooked his whim-worm—

slick, instructive, i poprocks like an art thot
bussy-blithe in vanity, unclean
machines me sterling pretty

what happening i mashy
he mashy. this slow, unwilling
succor i am funneled with dis-
ease…dripping

head to tow his dirty
worth. hi, bad
what power art thou

O putrid joy, unhomely
organs denuded to be

denied, the thing in the moment of the thing
i was living—all lols

blubber up down-home oh
sick plinth, anon in the open no
in my fuggo beefcake minefield

boom, bitch. a-quiver with—

he-device—clean metal predator
voided me filthy glottal

uh oh, homo lobo, uh oh

pudgy took it torquing
tradge, tradge

finger't like ally like thinging it throbbed all ontic

sported ago my own bornt derelick,   i cake it in
etceteretera, defang my repertoire

((ate a pill the size of i))
blech

i bus to the city to dance
with a man, merry as the market
accords us, statuses us, saddles us
up in dutiful intimacy. enter

the same flooding mammal tunnel
drunk on wonky wheels—i portal
for him, his random bunghole oculus, i
glitter swift horrif
                    love is not love is not

love. this is the fantasy—
in the damp & handsome muscle of earth, i let him
bury me. seed-bag. any hole can be a faggot
hole, i sing, *la la*. any ditch can be a faggot
ditch, he sings, *da dee*.

+ + +

what intimate monsters, what porous replicants
we are, sistered in secrecy, singing each other's songs
& oh the delight, & oh the false brush
of beauty, untethered from this
our volatile body

leaky phantoms levitate
tapping feelers upon me
garrot me nonstop

kissy—this is the fantasy, breeding
normal organism. i wore its placenta

with sentiment. i swore never again
then again overrode me

this is it, i say. i am alive
to this light. this is it, i say

then the metal on my back.

NOTES & ACKNOWLEDGMENTS

"glo-baude" adapts a couple short phrases from Jean Genet (translated by Bernard Frechtman), tarnishes Emily Dickinson's "everywhere of silver," warps a couple words from a Wayne Koestenbaum tweet, and draws inspiration from Kirsten Ihns.

"i fatten my fleet/ i pray for meat" adapts a phrase from Jean Genet (translated by Bernard Frechtman) and from drag queen DeAundra Peek.

"fleet week! cum manned me in the hows of warship" is a homophonic translation of T.S. Eliot's "Death by Water."

"depending on how you read a thing/ the ship is free, or it is sinking" adapts a couple short phrases from Hart Crane's "Voyages" and "The Broken Tower"; David Melnick's "Men in Aida"; Zeffirelli's *Romeo and Juliet*; and from various sea shanties. The title transforms a line in Deee-Lite's song, "Good Beat."

The second section of **"@melvillestomb"** is a homophonic translation of Hart Crane's "At Melville's Tomb" and transforms brief fragments of a 1924 letter to Waldo Frank about his romance with sailor Emil Opffer (found in *Hart Crane: Complete Poems & Selected Letters*, edited by Langdon Hammer, The Library of America, 2006). This poem takes inspiration from Meredith Stricker, adapts a phrase by William Blake, and warps one from Lara Glenum.

The word "horrif," which also appears in subsequent poems, is borrowed from Catherine Wagner.

"after the fall" is inspired by Hart Crane and Klaus Nomi.

"all gay ethic, eh?" (p. 21) is a f(r)agmented translation of Cavafy's "Morning Sea" working from the Greek and an English translation by Edmund Keeley and Philip Sherrard. The poem takes its title from David Melnick's *Men in Aida*.

"the fugacity of life's pleasures/ infatuate fatty cutlet" borrows a phrase from "The Rime of the Ancient Mariner" by Coleridge.

"♫butchered so nightly, yet love me♫" is a response to Cavafy's "Morning Sea." The text in black is comprised of a f(r)agmented translation of Aristophane's speech in Plato's *Symposium*.

"Atlantis" is an erasure-translation of Hart Crane's "Atlantis" from *The Bridge*. I derived the erasure through aleatory procedures, then added my own translation of "Atlantis" in gray. The poem adapts a couple short phrases from Pepper Mashay's "Dive in the Pool," as well as from Hito Steyerl's "Liquidity, Inc."

"on our first date he says he's poz & asks if i'm scared if i still wanna" adapts a soupçon of language from Anne Boyer, Julian Talamantez Brolaski, Cody-Rose Clevidence, Gerard Manley Hopkins, Heidi Lynn Staples, and Meredith Stricker.

"butch mercutio first time in drag at capulet ball" adapts a quip from Pete Zias.

"SISSY SESTINA 69" adapts a few words from Hart Crane, Klaus Nomi, and Walt Whitman.

"won't be the whole exclusive flesh won't be the marble like that" adapts a phrase from drag queen Dina Martina, transforms a short phrase from The B-52's "Dance This Mess Around," and warps a line from Hito Steyerl's essay "In Free Fall: A Thought Experiment on Vertical Perspective." The title is taken from *The Young and Evil* by Charles Henri Ford and Parker Tyler.

"all gay ethic, eh?" (p. 35) warps a soupçon of language from Georges Bataille's "Dream" and "The Solar Anus"; Carolyn Dean's *The Self and Its Pleasures*; Tim Dean's *Unlimited Intimacy*; Stan Hugill's *Shanties from the Seven Seas*; Derek McCormack's *The Well-Dressed Wound*; David Melnick's *Men in Aida*; Frank O'Hara's poem "for James Dean"; and Susan Sontag's essay "On Camp."

"amateur drag night/ a fucking didactic" sissies a line from Hart Crane's poem "The Wine Menagerie," ditties a little theory from Lee Edelman's *Homographesis*, and adapts a smidgen of language from drag queen Aja, some online wig stores, and the mid-aughts sitcom *Kath & Kim*.

"gently my joys distill/ lest you break the vessel you should fill" borrows a short phrase from Sir John Suckling and Hannah Weiner, and twists a line by Hart Crane.

"ship of fools" uses aleatory procedures to perform this erasure-translation of Hart Crane's "Voyages" (original text fragments seen in gray). The black text overlaid in sections 1–5 is my own translation of the text. Section six muddles a smidgen of language from the OED entry for the word "sissy," as well as from Derek McCormack's *The Well-Dressed Wound*. This poem transforms Doris Day and Bette Davis quotes, as well as twists a couple phrases from Lara Glenum, Walt Whitman, Catherine Wagner, and Hito Steyerl.

"if sometimes i seem not here, it's not dreaminess; it's fear" takes its title from a line by Kerri Webster, and adapts one from Hart Crane.

"s.o.s. girl overboa" is almost entirely comprised of the standard meanings of various international maritime signal flags from both the International Code of Signals and from NATO.

"in the navy" adapts a small bit of language from Cody-Rose Clevidence, Hart Crane, Tracey Emin, Quinn Morgendorfer, Catherine Wagner, & Laura Wetherington. This poem also adapts language from the OED entries for the words "sea," "fat," "faggot," "hole," "sailor."

"cold song" is partly inspired by Laura Wetherington's poem "The field is a blazon," and adapts a few words from David Melnick, Sara Jane Stoner, Catherine Wagner, and Henry Purcell's Cold Genius aria (as performed by Klaus Nomi).

Thank you to the editors of the following journals in which these poems originally appeared, sometimes in other forms, and sometimes with different titles:

Interim: "contam what lordly animates," "amateur drag night," "won't be the whole exclusive flesh won't be the marble like that"

Tampa Review: "the fugacity of life's pleasures/ infatuate, fatty cutlet!"

Sycamore Review: "depending on how you read a thing/ the ship is free, or it is sinking"

Apogee: "after the fall," "contam what lordly animates"

AADOREE: "@melvillestomb," "cold song," "ATLANTIS"

flag+void: "in the navy," "ye shing to war me/ har-harpoon"

jubilat: "all gay ethic, eh?"

TAGVVERK: "ship of fools"

New Delta Review: "on our first date he says he's poz & asks if i'm scared, if i still wanna"

Cloud Rodeo: "fleet week! cum manned me in the hows of warship," "gently my joys distill/ lest you break the vessel you should fill," "butchered so nightly, yet love me," "SISSY SESTINA 69"

SAND Journal: "glo-baude," "i fatten my fleet/ i pray for meat," "if sometimes i seem not here, it's not dreaminess; it's fear"

TINGE Magazine: "butch mercutio first time in drag at capulet ball"

Puerto del Sol: "buying spanx at the airport spanx store"

The following poems appeared in some form in my short chapbook *TANGLED BANK & daily bugaboo jubilee* (Letter [r] Press): "happy pride lol hole pic?"; "s.o.s. girl overboa"; "all gay ethic, eh?"; " ♫butchered so nightly, yet love me♫"; "daily bugaboo jubilee"; "butch mercutio first time in drag at capulet ball"; "buying spanx at the airport spanx store"

Utmost gratitude to my friends and Alabama family: Reem, Jordan, Rashanda, Julia, rb, Kayleb, Riley, Candystore, the BWR crew, and all the bird poets, especially Shaelyn, Ryan, and Zach.

A special thank you to my brilliant guides: Heidi Lynn Staples, Lamar Wilson, Emily Wittman, and Jennifer Purvis. Love and gratitude to Ken Mikolowski, John Ganiard, and Emma Claire Foley.

Thank you to everyone at the Cleveland State University Poetry Center for believing in this thing, especially Caryl Pagel, whose insight and support have been invaluable. A big big thank you to Hilary Plum and Sevy Perez as well.

& to Max, Michelle, and Rylie, stay cool ~

Shelley Feller is a former figure skater.
They live in Atlanta.

RECENT CLEVELAND STATE UNIVERSITY
POETRY CENTER PUBLICATIONS

Edited by Caryl Pagel & Hilary Plum

POETRY
World'd Too Much: The Selected Poetry of Russell Atkins
ed. Kevin Prufer and Robert E. McDonough
Advantages of Being Evergreen by Oliver Baez Bendorf
My Fault by Leora Fridman
Orient by Nicholas Gulig
Age of Glass by Anna Maria Hong
In One Form to Find Another by Jane Lewty
50 Water Dreams by Siwar Masannat
daughterrarium by Sheila McMullin
The Bees Make Money in the Lion by Lo Kwa Mei-en
Residuum by Martin Rock
Festival by Broc Rossell
Sun Cycle by Anne Lesley Selcer
Bottle the Bottles the Bottles the Bottles by Lee Upton

ESSAYS
I Liked You Better Before I Knew You So Well by James Allen Hall
A Bestiary by Lily Hoang
Codependence by Amy Long
The Leftovers by Shaelyn Smith

TRANSLATIONS
Scorpionic Sun by Mohammed Khaïr-Eddine, translated by Conor Bracken
I Burned at the Feast: Selected Poems of Arseny Tarkovsky translated by
Philip Metres and Dimitri Psurtsev

For a complete list of titles visit www.csupoetrycenter.com